If I Were a Fly on the Wall

Rose Barnes-Bey McLaurin
Kingdom Trailblazers Publishing

To my Grandma. I love you.

Introduction

Hello, my name is Rose Barnes-Bey McLaurin. I am a mother of four beautiful children. I have been a chef for over 20 years and a caterer for 10 of those years. I have written two other books: *Self Thoughts* (a dark poetry book) and *Easy, Simple, but Good Food* (a cookbook).

I decided to write this book about the ongoing issues in the restaurant industry that have been overlooked for years. This book is not intended to expose anyone or any company, but rather to enlighten you about what you are truly consuming. I have years of personal experience, and here are some of the realities I would love to share with you.

No company names or individuals have been listed in this book. There should be **three types of people** in the restaurant industry:

1. Those with strong communication skills.

Ideally, this should always be the case, but often, we experience the opposite. Orders are taken incorrectly—not always because the customer is unclear, but because the server may not truly care. Some are only there for the money, some are having a bad day and pass that energy on to the guest, and others were hired out of necessity and thrown into the job without proper training. They're overwhelmed, all over the place, and struggling to keep up. The same can happen in the kitchen. A cook may not read the ticket carefully, may feel underpaid, may be having a bad day, or may simply not care enough about the quality of the food being prepared.

2. Those who are quick and efficient. Speed and efficiency are essential, yet they're often lacking. Food can sit in the window dying while staff are talking, playing around, or eating—so by the time it reaches the table, it's cold. The cook didn't prepare it cold; it got cold because no one moved with urgency. Efficiency can be a stretch, because while some in the back of house care and some in the front of house care, not everyone takes responsibility for the guest's experience.

3. Those with a strong work ethic. You can always tell when someone truly cares. It shows in how the food is presented, how the server greets you, and how welcomed you feel when you walk through the door. It's in how amazing the food tastes and the overall experience you leave with. When people care about what they do, they take their time, pay attention to details, and give their best.

Table of Contents

1
Cold Food

Hey there - how are you today? Great, I hope. I've said it before, and I'll say it again: the world needs to know what they are putting in their mouths when they dine out. People complain every day about cold food, but very few understand *why* it happens. This chapter exists to clear that up.

First, let's be very clear. Your food is **not** cooked cold. That is the first assumption many guests make, and it's simply not true. No cook intentionally sends out cold food. When food comes out cold, the problem almost always happens *after* it has already been cooked.

One common reason is that the cook may have been "in the weeds," meaning overwhelmed and behind on orders. When this happens, food can sit too long before being placed under a heat lamp or before someone is ready to run it.

Second, some kitchens simply do not prioritize getting food into the window promptly. Once food is ready, seconds matter.

Third, and this is more common than people want to believe, servers may be in the back on their phones, talking, laughing, or eating while your food sits in the window dying. Every server knows they have less than a minute to run food to a guest. When they don't, the quality of your meal suffers.

2

Food vs. The Ads

Many people wonder why their food never looks like the marketing picture on the menu. I'm here to give you the answer.

In some cases, restaurants hire people simply because they need help, not because those individuals are properly trained. A person may need a job, and the restaurant is desperate to fill a position, so quality takes a back seat.

On busy nights, food is rushed onto the plate, the rim isn't clean, and the presentation is sloppy. Managers are tired. Staff are overwhelmed. Most of the time, nobody truly cares.

The pictures on menus are designed to draw you in. You've heard the saying, "You eat with your eyes first." These food tricks have been used since the early 1800s. Instead of focusing on the pictures, read the ingredients.

3

Did Someone Bite My Food

Someone touching your food is a major issue in the restaurant industry.

Imagine a cook pulling bread from a package, and the bottom half breaks off. The question becomes: waste food or save food cost? Most times, the broken piece is served, and the hope is that you won't notice.

Cooks generally do not eat directly off guest plates because they have access to food in the kitchen. Servers, however, are often picking off fries, nuggets, or anything easy to grab - hoping you don't pay attention.

4

Foreign Objects

This is one of the most disturbing realities in the restaurant industry, and it's something many people never want to think about until it happens to them.

A foreign object is anything in your food that does not belong there, such as hair, plastic, glass, insects, metal, nails, or any substance not listed as an ingredient.

These things do not appear by accident; they appear because of carelessness, lack of training, or people simply not following basic food safety rules.

Here's a real example: a cook wearing long, polished nails without gloves. One nail breaks off during service. No one notices where it went. That nail can easily end up in your soup, your pasta, or your sauce.

Dishwashers often use stainless-steel scrubbing pads. Over time, those pads shed metal fragments. Those fragments stay in pots, pans, grease, and fryers. When a cook is not paying attention, that metal transfers directly into your food.

Hair ends up in food because staff refuse to wear hair restraints or constantly touch their hair while cooking or serving. Plastic shows up when wrap isn't removed properly, glove tips break off, or containers are punctured instead of opened correctly.

Bugs get into food when doors are left open, patios are used without protection, lighting is poor, or pest control rules are ignored.

Here is the uncomfortable truth: some people truly do not care about what they are serving you. Always pray over your food, but if you see something wrong, do not eat it. No matter how much it costs, your health matters more.

5

Food Poisoning

People often ask this question after the damage has already been done. Food poisoning is not random; it usually comes from repeated bad practices inside the kitchen.

Food poisoning is an illness caused by bacteria, viruses, parasites, or toxins. One of the biggest causes is poor food rotation, also known as *first-in, first-out*. When this system is ignored, older food is pushed to the back, forgotten, and later served.

Instead of throwing spoiled food away, some kitchens will wash it off, soak it in milk to hide the smell, over-season it, fry it hard, or grill it aggressively to mask the taste and odor. This is done to avoid wasting money, not to protect your health.

At the end of the day, many places focus on selling the product and making money, not on what that food is doing to your body. If your food smells bad, has a strange taste, or feels questionable, do not eat it. No meal is worth risking your health.

6

Cooked Wrong

Undercooked food, especially poultry, pork, beef, and seafood, is dangerous. This can result from miscommunication, lack of training, or cooks simply not paying attention.

Overcooking happens when temperatures are too high or when food is left unattended. Pasta turns to mush, fish dries out, and rice becomes glue.

Under-seasoning may come from fear or inexperience. Over-seasoning often happens when cooks don't taste food or try to mask poor-quality ingredients.

7
Spoiled Food

This is one of those experiences people try to explain away, even when their instincts are telling them something is wrong.

If your food tastes spoiled or smells spoiled, most of the time it's because it *is* spoiled. Restaurants rely on customers second-guessing themselves, assuming it's the seasoning, the sauce, or just their imagination.

One major reason is improper refrigeration. Refrigerators may not be holding the correct temperature, or staff may overload them, preventing proper airflow. Food that is not cooled or stored correctly breaks down faster than people realize.

Another issue is improper storage. Someone may forget to refrigerate food after prep, or food may be stored uncovered, allowing contamination from other items. Cross-contamination is extremely common when raw and cooked foods are stored improperly.

Expired ingredients also play a role. Instead of throwing food away, some kitchens reheat it multiple times, hoping customers won't notice. Reheating old food changes its texture, smell, and taste, but many cooks take that chance anyway. Understaffing makes all this worse. When kitchens are rushed and poorly trained, food safety becomes an afterthought.

If your food smells off or tastes strange, do not eat it. Foods you should never eat spoiled include seafood, dairy products, cooked rice, sauces, leafy greens, pre-cut fruits, and meats. Trust your instincts.

8

Portion Problems

If you frequent the same restaurant, you may notice something strange over time: your favorite dish doesn't look the same anymore.

Portion inconsistency usually comes down to money. Food cost is one of the biggest expenses in a restaurant, and adjusting portion sizes is one of the easiest ways to increase profit without alerting customers.

Sometimes portions are increased to justify raising menu prices. Other times, portions quietly shrink while prices stay the same. The hope is that customers won't notice or won't say anything if they do.

Inconsistent portions can also result from poor training. Cooks may not be using measuring tools, or they may eyeball portions based on mood, rush, or laziness. One cook may give more, another less.

Management decisions also affect portions. Chefs or owners may instruct staff to reduce serving sizes during slow seasons or when food costs rise.

Next time you dine out, pay attention to portion sizes. Consistency tells you a lot about how a restaurant is being run.

9

Burnt Food

Burnt food is not always an accident. It's often a sign of deeper issues in the kitchen.

One common cause is incorrect cooking temperatures. Equipment such as ovens, grills, fryers, and flat-tops may be turned up too high to speed up service, especially during busy shifts.

Another reason is a lack of timing knowledge. Some cooks simply do not know proper cook times, or they walk away from food for too long because they are distracted or overwhelmed.

Food waste also plays a role. Instead of throwing food away and starting over, some restaurants send out burnt items just to get rid of them.

When burnt food is sent to your table, it sends a message; either no one was paying attention, or no one cared enough to fix it. Either way, you should pay attention.

10
Dirty Plates

A proper table setting should include clean plates, utensils, napkins, and glassware. When any of those items are dirty, it's a red flag.

Water stains, lipstick marks, and food particles usually come from dishwashing failures. Dishes may not be sprayed before being loaded into the dishwasher, or the machine itself may not be properly maintained.

Staffing issues also play a role. When restaurants are short-staffed, servers rush to reset tables, and dishwashers may be poorly trained or overwhelmed.

Improper stacking can smear food residue onto clean dishes, and servers may fail to inspect items before placing them on your table.

Napkins may arrive dirty from manufacturers yet still be used. Glasses may not be sanitized correctly. All these things point to a lack of standards.

If you notice dirty dishes, say something immediately. Cleanliness should never be optional.

11

Hands in My Food

This is an uncomfortable question, but it's one people ask for a reason.

Yes, hands end up in food more often than customers realize. Some staff eat from plates before they leave the kitchen. Others touch food without gloves or proper handwashing.

People working long shifts get hungry, careless, or curious, especially if the food looks good. Unfortunately, not everyone is stopped or corrected.

If you ever notice signs that someone has touched or eaten from your food, do not eat it. Take photos if necessary and report it to a manager.

Your health matters more than avoiding an awkward conversation.

12
Health Grades Exposed

Many people see a health inspection grade and assume it tells the full story of the restaurant. Unfortunately, that's not always true.

Health inspection grading systems vary by state, but they are generally based on local food codes. Some use letter grades, while others use point-based systems.

An A grade does not necessarily mean a restaurant is clean or free of violations. Inspectors may overlook issues, especially if they have relationships with the establishment.

A B grade indicates that violations were found and need correction. These may include temperature issues, improper food handling, dirty equipment, or lack of hair restraints and gloves.

A C grade is a serious warning. It can include violations such as a lack of hot water, cross-contamination, rodents, insects, standing water on floors, malfunctioning dishwashers, or improper handwashing facilities.

If issues are not corrected, restaurants can be shut down temporarily—or permanently.

The next time you see a health inspection grade; don't assume it guarantees safety. Take a closer look. Your health depends on it.

Conclusion

After everything you've read in this book, one thing should be clear: eating out is no longer as simple as placing an order and trusting that everything will be done correctly behind the scenes. Knowledge is your first line of defense.

This book was not written to scare you; it was written to prepare you. Restaurants are businesses first, and not all of them prioritize your health the way they should. That doesn't mean you should never eat out again, but it does mean you should eat out *aware*.

Pay attention to what you see, smell, and taste. Look at cleanliness, portion sizes, presentation, and how staff move and communicate. Trust your instincts. If something feels off, it probably is.

Speak up when something isn't right. Ask questions. Send food back if necessary. Walk away if you need to. No meal is worth compromising your health or peace of mind.

And finally, pray over your food. Not just out of habit, but with intention. Awareness plus prayer gives you discernment.

My hope is that after reading this book, you feel empowered—not afraid. Empowered to make informed decisions, protect yourself, and demand better from the places that serve you.

Because you deserve better.

About the Author

Rose Barnes-Bey McLaurin, a mother of four, is a chef, caterer, and author who finds fulfillment in sharing her life experiences through writing.

This book is a compelling read, offering insight into a range of real-life situations.